CFA Institute

LIQUIDITY IN EQUITY MARKETS

Characteristics, Dynamics, and Implications for Market Quality

CFA Institute is the global association of investment professionals that sets the standards for professional excellence. We are a champion for ethical behavior in investment markets and a respected source of knowledge in the global financial community.

Our mission is to lead the investment profession globally by promoting the highest standards of ethics, education, and professional excellence for the ultimate benefit of society.

ISBN: 978-1-942713-11-1
August 2015

Contents

Executive Summary

This paper provides the results of an investigation into two common practitioner complaints about modern equity markets. First, the perception is that modern market structure has created a set of incentives that increase adverse selection risk on pretrade transparent (or "lit") venues. Specifically, broker/dealer internalizers often execute the majority of uninformed retail order flow against their own principal, which can increase the probability that displayed limit orders on lit venues are executed only when these lit orders are on the wrong side of the trade (that is, against the direction of expected short-term market movements). For other market participants, this issue is worrying because the incentive to post lit orders is compromised. The result is to discourage from lit markets all but the most sophisticated traders, such as high-frequency traders (HFTs), who are able to manage adverse selection risks because of their speed advantage. Second, investment professionals are concerned that displayed liquidity is unrepresentative of the true ability to execute trades. The argument of these professionals is that HFTs post numerous duplicate limit orders to increase the probability of execution (or as part of some other strategy) because they know they have the speed advantage necessary to cancel the unnecessary duplicate orders before execution.

To understand the effects of these concerns on market quality, I studied the dynamics and characteristics of liquidity across equity markets in the United States, the United Kingdom, and France between 2010 and 2014. This study is a timely addition to the debate on the future of equity markets that is currently going on in the United States through the efforts of the SEC (Securities and Exchange Commission) and in the EU (European Union), where authorities are currently implementing the revised Markets in Financial Instruments Directive legislative package (MiFID II/MiFIR). Specifically, I investigated two related phenomena in the US, UK, and French equity markets. First, I examined the effect of adverse selection on lit markets by estimating the ability of electronic or OTC (over-the-counter) market makers (in a dealer capacity rather than a market-making capacity) to selectively route their own order flow to exchanges only when the market makers are on the right side of the trade. Electronic market makers are likely to be better informed about imminent "quote rolls," a phenomenon in which depth on one side of the order book is taken away by successive orders in a predictable manner until depth at the best price is exhausted and the quote rolls up or down. When the quote is stable, internalization is posited to be relatively highest, and OTC market makers deal profitably within the stable spread by leaning on the quotes posted on exchanges. When OTC market makers predict (based on either order-book imbalances or short-term price prediction algorithms) that the quote is about to roll, they route their own orders to exchanges and trade in the direction of expected price changes (being on the "right" side of the trade). In this way, displayed liquidity providers are adversely selected against; they end up on the wrong side of the trade because more "informed" orders are routed to lit exchanges. By measuring the proportions of off-exchange or "dark" trading during periods when the quote is stable and when it is rolling (i.e., nonstable), I could investigate the extent to which limit orders on lit venues are adversely selected against.

Second, I considered the extent to which depth at the top of the order book may be made up of duplicate liquidity by examining the impact of a trade on the order-book depth in terms of a multiple of the trade size. If there is no systematic duplication of limit orders, a trade of a given size is posited to have an impact on the depth in the order book equal to its size. That is, when a trade is executed for 100 shares, top-of-the-book depth will decrease by 100 shares as a direct result of the trade (the time was defined as within 50 milliseconds), not by, say, 300 shares.

This study found evidence consistent with adverse selection on lit markets being made worse by traders executing inside the spread during stable quote periods before executing against lit venues when the quote is unstable. This finding is a clear example of traders interacting with lit venues more when they are better informed. This study did not find any evidence in any market consistent with trades having an outsize impact on order-book depth, which would suggest systematic liquidity duplication. However, I documented some evidence that liquidity is replaced increasingly slowly on the main UK lit exchange.

The policy implications of these findings centre on the differences in results between the US markets, on the one hand, and UK and French markets on the other hand. The US markets provide trade-through protection, retail order flow internalization, and fixed tick sizes (or minimum price variation, also known as MPV). The UK and French markets have no trade-through protection, less extensive retail order flow internalization, and more variation in tick sizes. Specifically, the fixed US tick size (MPV is 1 cent for all stocks priced above USD1.00) may be hampering the ability of very liquid US stocks to achieve a true equilibrium price, which may explain why the proportion of trading in dark venues approximately doubles during periods when the quote is stable. In other words, liquidity may be constrained from amassing at equilibrium price levels on exchanges and is channeled into dark venues where subpenny execution is possible. Recalibration of tick size policy to allow smaller ticks for more liquid stocks may be a way to reduce this phenomenon and thereby limit adverse selection. This study found some evidence of the adverse selection phenomenon on certain exchanges in the UK market, although the effect is not as uniformly strong or statistically significant as in the US market. In the French market, I struggled to find enough examples of stable quote periods to make any meaningful statistical inference, which, in itself, is an interesting result. I could not determine (from this analysis) whether this result is a cause or a consequence of the lower degree of internalization in France than in, for example, the United States.

The incentives in the US markets appear to generate behaviour that is consistent with increased adverse selection on lit venues. In contrast, the UK and French markets, with their different market structures, do not appear to see this behaviour to the same extent, if at all. This dichotomy should be an input into the debate on future market structure on both sides of the Atlantic.

1. Introduction

Historically, liquidity in equity markets came from a variety of sources, including traditional market makers, floor specialists, floor locals,[1] institutions, day traders, and retail investors. This diversified provision of liquidity came from parties with different goals, investment horizons, and trading strategies. Although markets have periodically endured significant traumas, such as the 1987 market crash, during most periods, markets have enjoyed a regular supply of interest from different types of buyers and sellers.

The nature and the sources of liquidity started to change at the turn of the millennium. In US equity markets, the significant changes began with demutualization and decimalization in the late 1990s and continued, in 2006, with Regulation National Market System (Reg NMS), which opened up the exchange industry to competition. Other global markets experienced similar changes, most notably in Europe following the introduction of the Markets in Financial Instruments Directive (MiFID) in 2007. As a result of Reg NMS and MiFID, as well as constant improvements in technology, trading has become increasingly automated, fast paced, competitive, and fragmented among listing venues. This evolution has been accompanied by a decrease in average trade size and a significant increase in overall quote traffic and transaction volumes. Direct trading costs (both bid–ask spreads and commissions) have generally fallen,[2] whereas liquidity has become increasingly dispersed among multiple venues and the provision of liquidity has become driven by an increasingly homogenous set of market participants—algorithmic or high-frequency traders (HFTs).[3]

These changes have been blamed for creating incentives that are perceived to have increased the risk of adverse selection on lit markets and reduced the resilience of liquidity supply. The first issue—adverse selection—may be caused either by informed traders self-selecting onto lit venues or uninformed traders self-selecting away from lit venues. In both cases, the consequence is that a market maker on a lit venue is more likely to be interacting with an informed trader than an uninformed trader and thus be on the wrong

[1]Floor specialists and locals are mostly a US phenomenon; European markets have been fully electronic since the mid-1980s.

[2]Direct trading costs comprise bid–ask spreads and commissions; indirect trading costs include market impact and delay costs as well as unrealized profit from unexecuted trades. The evidence regarding trends in indirect trading costs is ambiguous.

[3]The distinction between algorithmic and high-frequency trading is not meaningful at this time because most algorithmic traders operate at a high frequency and most HFTs use algorithms.

side of the trade. The market maker has to increase her bid–ask spread to compensate for the increased probability of losing money to informed traders.

The second issue—market liquidity—may have several interpretations. The technical definitions of liquidity include *breadth of the market*, which is measured by the width of the bid–offer spread, and *depth of the market*, measured by quantities available on the bid and the offer at the top of the order book as well as through the order book. Related to this issue, however, is the resilience of the market, measured by market impact, or the ability of the market to absorb orders without moving the price. Anecdotally, many buy-side institutions, market makers, and other market participants have raised concerns about the ability of modern markets to absorb institutional-sized orders. Whether these concerns are justified by data-driven evidence is being debated. This study should be seen as a contribution to this debate.

The intention is to provide a snapshot of the state of market liquidity according to all of the preceding definitions. Relative to extant literature, this study contributes an analysis of both US and European (UK and French) markets during overlapping periods and provides a practitioner-based approach to examining adverse selection and liquidity resilience in equity markets.

2. Literature Review

This section presents a review of key contributions to the literature related to the impact of market structure developments on liquidity and market quality. The first group of papers deals with the impact of market fragmentation as a result of Reg NMS and MiFID. This discussion motivates the next section, which addresses the increase in automated high-frequency trading (HFT). This section is followed by a detailed discussion of the two main types of HFTs—passive and aggressive. The literature review concludes with findings from research on the stability of liquidity provision in modern markets.

2.1. Market Impact of Visible Fragmentation

Reg NMS and MiFID opened up the exchange industry to increased competition by allowing trading in securities outside the listing venue. The rise of new trading venues caused a partial but significant shift of trading from mostly lit venues, which are pretrade transparent, to dark venues, which are pretrade opaque. Dark venues allow traders to bypass queues at the top of the book on lit venues, receive greater execution certainty in the dark, and reduce the market impact of their (invisible prior to execution) large trades.

Increased competition between lit venues (visible fragmentation) has generally been found to have a beneficial effect on liquidity (Degryse, De Jong, and van Kervel 2015) in the form of reduced trading costs and improved market quality, but the consequences of increased dark trading are mixed. The benefits of increased dark trading appear to derive from increased competition among equity markets, whereas the disadvantages arise as a result of adverse selection (see Preece and Rosov 2014 for more details). Specifically, dark trading tends to result in more informed or "toxic" order flow on lit venues because uninformed order flow self-selects onto dark venues. This process may cause an increase in adverse selection on lit venues, which can disincentivise displayed liquidity provision.

2.2. Algorithmic Trading and HFTs

The rise in fragmented electronic-order-book markets has encouraged the development of algorithmic trading (AT) systems that can aggregate and act on information from multiple exchanges much more quickly than human traders. In the place of traditional market activities and participants is a structure dominated by HFT, payment for order flow arrangements that supply broker/dealer internalization networks,[4] and dark pools. HFT is a subset of AT; the algorithms involved in HFT have a different focus. To distinguish HFT from AT, the SEC (2014) lists five characteristics of HFT:

1. Use of high-speed programs for generating, routing, and executing orders
2. Use of co-location services to minimise network latencies
3. Very short holding periods
4. Submission of numerous orders that are cancelled shortly after submission
5. Not holding inventory positions overnight

Different types of HFT are likely to have different effects on equity markets. HFT is commonly classified according to strategy type, trade aggressiveness (i.e., liquidity taking versus liquidity supplying), and latency level (i.e., speed).

Among strategy types, the SEC (2014) identifies four categories:

1. Passive market-making strategies (liquidity-supplying strategies that earn profits by capturing the bid–offer spread and/or liquidity rebates paid by exchanges)
2. Arbitrage strategies, which profit from correcting short-lived market inefficiencies—specifically, mispricing of similar securities and financial instruments across markets
3. Structural strategies, which seek to exploit market infrastructure and network latencies; examples include controversial "quote stuffing" strategies (sending a large number of messages to exchange servers that overwhelm the system and thereby create stale prices for other traders) and predatory "order-sniffing" strategies (liquidity detection algorithms that move prices across venues up or down ahead of institutional investors' orders)
4. Directional strategies, which profit from triggering a sudden price movement; momentum ignition strategies, for example, aim to profit by sending a series of orders and trades in an attempt to quickly run up or run down the market price

The various HFT strategies likely have differing impacts on market quality. For example, although market-making strategies are typically liquidity providing and thus generally

[4]Payment for order flow is not allowed in the United Kingdom.

beneficial for market quality, structural and directional strategies are typically liquidity taking and may be associated with volatility. Some of the commonly cited concerns regarding the market impact of HFT are as follows:

1. The perception that HFT market makers supply "fair weather" liquidity that can and will vanish quickly during adverse market conditions

2. Crowding out at the National Best Bid and Offer (NBBO) level, where execution certainty at the top of the book declines as a result of marketable order flow being routed away from lit venues by brokers trying to avoid paying access fees and dark venues offering price improvement relative to the NBBO

3. Phantom liquidity, in which traders are not able to execute quantities advertised in the order book because the posted limit orders providing liquidity are cancelled before they can be executed against

4. Latency arbitrage, in which HFTs take advantage of communication delays between exchanges within the market infrastructure

5. Maker-taker fee prioritization, in which trading and quoting decisions are based primarily on optimising exchange rebates and fees

2.3. Market Impact of HFT Market Makers

Of the HFT strategy types discussed in the previous section, the most important distinction is between passive market-making strategies and the others, which could be grouped together as aggressive strategies. The differences in behaviour and consequences of these two types of HFT are very important, and any discussion of HFTs must be clear about which of these HFT types is being discussed.

The literature often concludes that the rise of HFTs has been good for liquidity and market quality—with a reduction in spreads and increase in liquidity (see, for example, Jovanovic and Menkveld 2011; Bershova and Rakhlink 2013). However, this effect cannot be attributed to HFTs as a homogenous group. The mechanism driving this liquidity improvement is likely that passive HFT strategies have largely taken over the role of market making (see Menkveld 2013). HFT market makers are able to quickly submit and cancel a large number of orders, so they are less likely to be executed against by informed traders, which reduces their adverse selection risk and allows them to quote tight spreads.

Although HFT market makers may improve market quality by intermediating trades at a reduced cost, they may also use their speed to disadvantage other investors and increase adverse selection costs, which reduces market quality (Jones 2013).

2.4. Adverse Selection: Impact of Aggressive HFTs

The market impact of aggressive HFTs is controversial. On the one hand, aggressive HFTs are found to be associated with improvements in price discovery (see, for example, Brogaard, Hendershott, and Riordan 2013; Carrion 2013), which leads to more efficient prices and an improvement in market quality. This effect is observed mostly for large-capitalisation stocks, in which the bulk of HFT occurs.

On the other hand, the information advantage that aggressive HFTs have over other market participants is very short term—measured in fractions of a second. Zhang (2012) found that in the long run, passive non-HFTs consistently demonstrate a higher contribution to price discovery (see also SEC 2014). The gain in price efficiency from aggressive HFT strategies, therefore, may not outweigh potential adverse selection costs.

Adverse selection may manifest itself in a number of ways, but the basic idea is that HFTs (and modern market structure in general) cause the order flow on lit exchanges to be relatively more informed and thereby more toxic for market makers, resulting in wider spreads. Consider, for example, a stock trading at 20.00–20.01 at the NBBO. HFT internalizers (i.e., off-exchange market makers operating at a high frequency) can fill incoming retail marketable buy orders at 20.0099 (in front of the displayed offer) and fill all retail marketable sell orders at 20.0001 (in front of the displayed bid), which results in a nominal price improvement of 0.0001 in each case. In this example, the HFT market makers would earn the spread minus the nominal price improvement.

Now, consider market makers who post visible limit orders. Their orders generally do not interact with uninformed retail order flow—which is always being internalized. Where does that leave these market makers? They are trading with relatively more informed order flow and, therefore, are more likely to be on the wrong side of a trade—that is, face increased adverse selection risk. Hendershott and Mendelson (2000) found evidence consistent with this idea when they examined orders being routed to the lit market after failing to execute in a midpoint crossing system. Using the lit market as a "market of last resort" in this way leads to order flow imbalances, which increases inventory and adverse selection risks, and harms liquidity. Brogaard et al. (2013) also found evidence that HFTs impose adverse selection costs on other investors on the NYSE and NASDAQ.

Based on these findings, my first hypothesis is that relatively more trades will execute off-exchange when the quotes are stable and that displayed limit orders on exchanges will be executed against relatively more when the quotes change or "roll." What is happening is that internalizers are causing trades to happen inside the quote by offering price improvement (as described previously). When they see order imbalances that predict that the quote is about to roll, they neutralize their net positions by executing against the lit quote.

For example, if the HFT internalizers have a net long position just before a quote rolls down, they will seek to sell at the bid in the expectation that they will imminently be able to repurchase at the (lower) future ask price. In the US market, this practice should appear in the consolidated tape as a series of off-exchange trades executed at the NBBO and then an on-exchange trade just as the quote rolls. In this way, HFT internalizers are liquidity providers when quotes are stable but liquidity takers when quotes roll; the posted quote is acting merely as insurance for this strategy.

This scenario is a strikingly clear example of adverse selection in action: HFT internalizers are mopping up uninformed retail order flow and interacting with lit orders only when the lit orders are on the wrong side of the trade. For other market participants, this scenario is worrying because the incentive to post lit orders is compromised. All but the most sophisticated traders (such as HFTs, who are best able to manage their risk exposure to adverse selection) are discouraged from posting limit orders in the lit markets.

Bid–ask spreads are the most obvious way to measure trading costs, but price impact is often more important for large block orders that have to be "worked" (Jones 2013). Implementation shortfall is a way of measuring these institutional trading costs and is calculated as the return achieved from trading using the actual prices and traded quantities compared with the return on a notional portfolio consisting of the original trade size executed in full against the market price at the time the decision to trade was taken. Tong (2013) found that a 1 standard deviation increase in HFT activity increases the implementation shortfall by a third. He argued that HFT represents an ephemeral and expensive source of liquidity.

Jones (2013) noted, however, that institutional trading costs have declined during the rise of HFT, so costs related to implementation shortfall—price slippage and unrealized trade costs—appear to be economically unimportant when set against the decline in overall trading costs.

Another way of looking at this issue is the profitability of HFTs. Hendershott, Jones, and Menkveld (2011) estimated the gross average trading revenue of 25 of the largest HFTs to be USD2,351 per stock per day, which Jones (2013) noted is a fraction of the revenues earned by specialists 15 years ago.

A recent attempt to address the issue of adverse selection is the introduction of price improvement rules in Canada and Australia. The rules, essentially, require dark trades to provide price improvement on displayed quotations of 1 tick (or half a tick if the bid–offer spread is 1 tick).

Foley and Putnins (2014) investigated the experience of the Canadian and Australian markets and found relatively little evidence in favour of price improvement or so-called trade-at rules. Specifically, although the volume of dark trading fell after the implementation of the rule, this effect did not appear to have a positive impact on market quality measures. First, they found no evidence that lit limit order posting increased. Second, spreads and price impact actually increased. The authors argue that the reason is probably that in a market where many stocks have spreads of 1 tick (i.e., they are constrained by tick size), a price improvement rule of 1 tick necessarily means that the only price improvement dark venues can provide is to execute at the midpoint. However, the conversion of dark markets from two-sided markets into midpoint-by-default crossing venues likely self-selects more uninformed order flow onto dark markets (Zhu 2014), leaving relatively more informed order flow on lit venues. This toxic order flow causes market makers to face increased adverse selection costs, which may explain why spreads were observed to increase.[5]

2.5. Stability of Liquidity

Apart from the issue of adverse selection on lit venues and its associated explicit impact on costs, a concern is that liquidity in modern markets is not as stable as it once was. Whether the potential benefits of HFT, such as observed lower spreads and higher liquidity, are persistent or will disappear during times of market breakdowns is unclear. The issues are summarised by Jones's (2013) question: "Does HFT make markets more fragile?"

Flash Crash

The flash crash of 6 May 2010 is often put forward as an example that markets have become fragile in recent times. Several studies of the flash crash (for example, Kirilenko,

[5]CFA Institute has previously recommended that internalization of retail orders be required to offer meaningful price improvement in order to generate economically meaningful savings for retail investors and also to provide some protection to investors posting displayed orders in limit order books.

Kyle, Samadi, and Tuzun 2014) suggest, however, that HFT was not the proximate cause. In fact, it appears that HFT contributed stabilising liquidity into the market before being overwhelmed by selling pressure that caused HFTs to also change their strategies and liquidate their positions. Jones (2013) noted that a similar flash crash happened in 1962 and concluded that the likely cause of the 1962 flash crash was the human reaction to step aside when markets change suddenly rather than anything related to HFT in particular.

The effect of market fragmentation on the flash crash was examined by Madhavan (2012). He studied quote fragmentation—the extent to which multiple trading venues quote at the best prices—and found that higher quote fragmentation was associated with larger price moves during the flash crash.

Gao and Mizrach (2013) found, however, that the flash crash was not an isolated event. They analysed stock movements that would trip the new (post-flash crash) circuit-breaker regulations (i.e., a price decline of 10% or more followed by a recovery of at least 2.5%). The authors found that the incidence of these market quality breakdowns has been reducing (on average) since the mid-1990s and that 2010, despite the flash crash and the rise of HFT, had the fewest breakdowns in recent years. However, their empirical results suggest that HFT exacerbates these market quality breakdowns by causing correlation among market orders in different stocks.

SEC Rule 611, the trade-through rule, may also have been a contributing factor to the flash crash. Although Rule 611 ensures that trades are routed to the venue with the best price, it does so only for the top of the book. For example, if an order is sent to NYSE Arca, Arca must route that order to any other exchanges that are at the top of the book (SEC Rule 611 protection). But after the top of the book is satisfied, the remainder of the order can be routed to any exchange, even if there are better quotations on exchanges not chosen. In essence, better quotes can be traded through as long as they are not at the top of the book. Discussions with market practitioners suggest that many of the mini-flash crashes observed today may be caused by Rule 611 not providing protection to depth quotations.

Other Events

The issue of liquidity stability outside the flash crash was investigated by Alampieski and Lepone (2011), who found evidence for the resilience of HFT participation during periods of heightened adverse selection. Specifically, they investigated HFT activity in 2010 on the consolidated UK market (London Stock Exchange, or LSE, and BATS Chi-X

Europe) in response to US macroeconomic data announcements. They found that HFTs increase their participation around the macro news announcements whereas non-HFTs reduce their participation. Although HFT liquidity demand increases immediately around the news announcement, liquidity supply is significantly higher before and after the announcement relative to non-HFTs.

Furthermore, their results show that HFTs increase their liquidity provision to non-HFTs during the announcement period because non-HFTs leave the market and HFT depth reversion occurs faster than that of non-HFTs. This result is to be expected because HFTs are able to manage their risk exposure by constantly adjusting their liquidity supply, in contrast to traditionally slower market makers, who typically manage risk by exiting the order book. HFTs will always be quicker than other market participants to cancel these orders or "get out of the way" once information is revealed.

2.6. Summary

A brief summary of the extant literature on market structure and the effects of dark trading and HFT on market quality follows:

- Competition and fragmentation among pretrade transparent venues is good for market quality.
- Fragmentation of trading between lit and dark venues is beneficial up to a point but will eventually likely be a disincentive for liquidity provision.
- High-frequency market makers appear to be generally beneficial for markets.
- High-frequency aggressive trading strategies have mixed effects on market quality that trade off improved price efficiency for increased adverse selection.
- The net result of all of these effects has been an observed decrease in explicit trading costs and increase in liquidity, although questions remain about the resilience of this liquidity.

Adverse selection is a key issue determining investor behaviour in terms of how and where to execute orders. Adverse selection risk drives the determination to participate or not in lit markets, and the ability to manage this risk depends on speed (the ability to adjust quotes before being executed against when on the wrong side of the market). HFT allows traders to efficiently manage this risk but makes it difficult for non-HFTs to participate as market makers in modern markets, which increases the market's reliance on HFT liquidity provision. The stability of this liquidity has been debated and requires further examination.

The next sections provide an innovative, practitioner-based analysis of the issue of adverse selection and liquidity stability to shed more light on the nature of modern liquidity.

3. Data

The markets chosen for this study differ in several ways that are important for any analysis of liquidity. On the one hand, the US market comprises 12 registered exchanges that feed their order book data into a consolidated tape via the Securities Information Processor (SIP).[6] This structure, together with trade-through protection for best quotations, results in a virtually unified market. On the other hand, the European markets benefit neither from a single consolidated tape nor from trade-through protection. Each trading venue is, therefore, more autonomous (on a millisecond basis) than the US market.

The practice of retail order flow internalization via payment for order flow is also more developed in the United States. In the EU, the practice of internalization is more tightly regulated under MiFID. Systematic internalizers generally trade in relatively small sizes with either retail or professional customers (or both) and are required to publish quotes only for trades up to "standard" market size in "liquid" markets, as defined under MiFID. So, a limited degree of pretrade transparency exists around internalization in Europe, although the absence of a consolidated tape, together with the ability of systematic internalizers to be selective about who sees their quotes, means that, in practice, the transparency of internalization is somewhat similar in both regions. Therefore, a comparison of the regions is valid, but we should not expect the same results because of the differing structures. In particular, the adverse selection impact of HFTs in lit European markets may be reduced by the market structure in the EU. Finally, note that the non-US markets were chosen, in part, because of data availability.

3.1. European Data

Data for the UK and French markets are from IFS LiquidMetrix in raw exchange message form. Data on quotes and trades were collected for the periods described in **Exhibit 1**.

The sample period shown in Exhibit 1 (broadly 2010–2014) is based on the ideas in Alampieski and Lepone (2011). For each calendar month, two days of data were collected. The first is the day of the US nonfarm payroll data release, which is typically the first Friday of the month. The second set of data is from five calendar days after the nonfarm payroll announcement (typically the following Wednesday). Data availability largely dictated the sample selection (and the exceptions listed).

[6]For more information on SIP and trade reporting in the United States, see Section 2 of Preece (2012).

Exhibit 1. Sample Period Selection

Venue		United Kingdom	France	United States
LSE	2014	Jan–Dec excl. Jun	—	—
	2012	Jan–Jul excl. Apr	—	—
	2010	Jun–Dec	—	—
Chi-X	2014	Jan–Dec excl. Jun	Jan–Dec excl. Jun	—
	2012	Jan–Jul excl. Apr	Jan–Jul excl. Apr	—
	2010	Jun–Dec	—	—
BATS Europe	2014	Jan–Dec excl. Jun	Jan–Dec excl. Jun	—
	2012	Jan–Jul excl. Apr	Jan–Jul excl. Apr	—
	2010	Jun–Dec	—	—
Turquoise	2014	Jan–Dec excl. Jun	Jan–Dec excl. Jun	—
	2012	Jan–Jul excl. Apr	Jan–Jul excl. Apr	—
	2010	Jun–Dec	—	—
Euronext	2014	—	Jan–Dec excl. Jun	—
	2012	—	Jan–Jul excl. Apr	—
	2010	—	—	—
United States	2014			Jan–Dec excl. Jun
	2012	—	—	—
	2011	—	—	Jan–May
	2010	—	—	Jun–Dec
	2004	—	—	Jan–Dec
	1999	—	—	Jan–Dec excl. Apr

Note: Chi-X, BATS Europe, and Turquoise are common to both the UK and French markets. US data are from the 12 exchanges that feed their data to the consolidated quote and tape system SIP.

For each day, data were collected from the BATS, Turquoise, and Chi-X trading venues (three of the largest pan-European trading venues). Additionally, for UK stocks, I collected data from the LSE and, for French stocks, data from Euronext (the primary listing venues for the two respective markets).

For the UK and French markets, I isolated quote and trading data on 50 stocks split evenly into 25 large-cap and 25 small-cap groups (data are available from the author). The order book for each exchange was constructed for the top five levels at every instance in time (time stamped to the millisecond) and retained data only for the trading hours of 08:00–16:30 GMT.

3.2. US Data

Tick Data provided US market data in raw exchange message form for the dates described in Exhibit 1. Data on quotes and trades for the years 2010–2014 were selected to overlap as much as possible with the UK/French data. The US data are from the SIP, so only the top-level order-book data are available.

4. Descriptive Statistics

This section presents the descriptive statistics for the UK, French, and US markets examined in this study.

4.1. UK Market

The descriptive statistics shown in **Exhibit 2** were censored or winsorized at the 2% level so that any data above the 98th percentile were set equal to the value of the 98th percentile. The data presented in Exhibit 2 are for the UK equity market, comprising the LSE, Turquoise, BATS, and Chi-X trading venues.

The row labeled "Dark percent" is the proportion of venue trading that is reported as being off-exchange. The definition of a dark, or pretrade nontransparent, trade is from the list of trade types reported by each venue, and the statistics are a proportion of total trading on that particular venue. These statistics are affected by the dominant LSE, which has no dark trading.[7] As a percentage of all trades, both large-cap and small-cap stocks have seen dark trades rise from 4.5%–5.5% in 2010 to 6.5%–7.5% in 2014. When the descriptive statistics were calculated by exchange (not shown), Turquoise and BATS switched places as the leading dark venues between 2010 and 2014 (with dark trading accounting for around 14% of trades for BATS in 2014), and Chi-X grew from around 4% of trades being dark to around 7.5%.

Note also that dark trading in the United Kingdom is reported via the venues themselves, not a consolidated trade-reporting facility as in the United States. The effect is that dark trades on, for example, Turquoise, comprise both dark trades executed on the Turquoise system as well as off-exchange trades reported to Turquoise but not necessarily executed on Turquoise systems. This should not have an impact on the study because I did not conduct an analysis by venue. The incumbent reporting venue for off-exchange dark trades at the start of the sample period was Markit BOAT. This facility was responsible for a large proportion of off-exchange trade reporting prior to 2014, but these data are not in the sample. BOAT data may suffer from issues with accuracy of the time stamp relative to the millisecond-by-millisecond tick data from the exchanges, as well as potential double-counting in BOAT trade data. These factors limited the

[7]Note that the LSE owns Turquoise, which operates a separate dark order book that accounted for a significant portion of dark trading in the United Kingdom in this study.

Exhibit 2. Descriptive Statistics for UK Data

	2010		2012		2014	
Statistic	Large Cap	Small Cap	Large Cap	Small Cap	Large Cap	Small Cap
Relative spread (bps)						
Mean	8.43	43.95	8.65	40.13	7.63	47.04
Median	6.75	38.03	7.05	31.92	5.93	53.99
Std. dev.	6.63	25.49	6.85	23.77	6.21	18.78
Depth-weighted spread (bps)						
Mean	14.71	73.70	15.37	75.60	13.52	55.67
Median	10.89	76.43	11.51	84.26	10.74	58.11
Std. dev.	12.85	32.83	12.40	21.83	9.97	6.29
Effective spread (bps)						
Mean	6.10	17.80	5.74	17.70	5.05	29.60
Median	4.89	16.07	4.61	15.08	3.77	29.32
Std. dev.	5.47	11.56	5.59	11.76	6.23	16.31
Depth at top of book						
Mean	4,815	2,546	4,337	2,496	3,040	3,123
Median	2,265	1,412	1,571	1,290	1,357	1,597
Std. dev.	6,750	3,744	6,587	3,988	4,050	4,216
Depth (GBP value) at top of book						
Mean	24,308.00	6,306.84	23,116.63	4,213.79	24,956.27	4,207.25
Median	18,420.43	4,112.94	16,293.48	2,734.80	17,177.67	2,409.42
Std. dev.	20,273.05	7,268.66	21,901.47	4,876.43	23,887.11	5,824.15
Trade size						
Mean	1245	1086	898	859	607	1199
Median	473	396	291	340	272	689
Std. dev.	2129	1972	1699	1534	857	1304
Number of trades per day						
Mean	2,190	178	2,564	197	2,299	81
Median	1,335	56	1,637	51	1,626	33
Std. dev.	1,983	277	1,931	248	2,525	145

(continued)

Exhibit 2. Descriptive Statistics for UK Data (continued)

Statistic	2010 Large Cap	2010 Small Cap	2012 Large Cap	2012 Small Cap	2014 Large Cap	2014 Small Cap
Quote-to-trade ratio						
Mean	60.883	248.225	38.583	128.342	28.651	74.191
Median	46.921	132.16	33.734	77.125	25.031	48.145
Std. dev.	41.114	534.053	17.663	160.06	14.752	79.588
Dark percent						
Mean	6.14%	8.62%	5.36%	9.18%	6.82%	10.27%
Median	4.27	5.41	5.45	5.57	6.87	7.37
Std. dev.	6.22	10.74	3.97	10.63	5.42	10.96

Note: Statistics are presented by market capitalisation with membership of each group determined by the FTSE subindex in which the stock trades. The depth-weighted spread is calculated on the basis of executing an order for GBP25,000 worth of stock.

usefulness of BOAT data in this study. For this reason, I used only trade data reported by the exchange venues sampled. Discussions with practitioners suggest that including BOAT data would result in the total proportion of dark trading increasing from 6%–7% to 12%–13%.

Exhibit 2 indicates that relative spreads for large-cap stocks declined from 6.5–7.0 bps in 2010–2012 to closer to 6 bps in 2014. In contrast, the relative spread for small-cap stocks increased, particularly since 2012, from the mid-30s bps to about 55 bps.

The effective spread measures the actual spreads paid in executed transactions[8] and shows a similar trend to relative spreads in Exhibit 2. Effective spreads for large-cap stocks appear to be approximately 1 bp less than relative spreads, however, which is consistent with many large-cap trades receiving price improvement. Small-cap effective spreads are approximately half of the relative spread, which may be a result, again, of off-exchange execution with price improvement.

The depth-weighted relative spread measure simulated the execution of a GBP25,000 buy or sell order. The effective bid–offer spread was calculated on the quantities available at

[8]Specifically, the effective spread is calculated as the price paid minus the midpoint at the time of the trade. This amount is then multiplied by 2 to get a round-trip effective spread.

each price level until the order was exhausted. The result is approximately double that of the relative spread discussed previously, with large-cap stocks having a depth-weighted effective spread of 10.5–11.5 bps (with no discernible trend since 2010) and small-cap stocks similarly showing no obvious trend but ultimately falling from 75 bps to 58 bps between 2010 and 2014.

The median depth at the top of the book has experienced a linear decline from 2,250 shares to about 1,350 shares for large-cap stocks. A small increase can be observed for small-cap stocks (from 1,400 shares to about 1,600 shares). These figures are effectively per-venue medians, so it also makes sense to consider the mean, which will be skewed by the large depth on the LSE (approximately double that of the depth on Chi-X, Turquoise, or BATS) and, therefore, be more representative in this case. The mean depth has also declined—from about 5,000 shares to about 3,000 shares. The depth in value terms for large-cap stocks has been quite stable, with approximately GBP24,000 worth of depth (mean) across all years. Interestingly, unlike small-cap depth in shares, small-cap depth in value terms has decreased from just over GBP6,000 in 2010 to just over GBP4,000 in 2014.

In summary, the descriptive statistics for the United Kingdom tell us a few stylized facts:

- Dark trading as a proportion of all trading has increased by 1.5–2.0 percentage points.
- Large-cap relative spreads have stayed relatively stable whereas small-cap spreads have increased on both a relative and effective basis; small-cap depth-weighted spreads, however, have fallen. Effective spreads tend to be lower than relative spreads, which is consistent with trades being executed with price improvement.
- Institutional trades (GBP25,000) cost approximately double the relative spread.
- Depth at the top of the book has fallen in both share and value terms for large-cap stocks and in value terms for small-cap stocks.
- Trade sizes have fallen for large-cap stocks but increased for small-cap stocks.

The descriptive statistics are consistent with a market that has experienced no significant developments or improvements in market quality in the large-cap sector since 2010 but experienced deterioration in some market quality measures for small-cap stocks.

4.2. French Market

The French markets, shown in **Exhibit 3**, look quite similar to the UK markets—with large-cap relative spreads of 5–6 bps (specifically, dropping from 6.2 to 5.2 bps between 2012 and 2014). Small-cap spreads appear to be lower than in the United Kingdom—about 10 bps. Effective spreads are lower than relative spreads, 3–4 bps for large-cap stocks and 5–8 bps for small-cap stocks, which, again, reflects the execution of trades with price improvement. The depth-weighted spread is also much closer to the relative spread for both large- and small-cap stocks when compared with the United Kingdom, implying that French equity markets are better able to absorb large institutional orders (EUR25,000 or more). Note also, however, that the depth-weighted measure in the United Kingdom executes a trade of GBP25,000, which is worth more than EUR25,000.

Top-of-book depth is, as in the UK markets, skewed, and in this case, by the dominance of Euronext, which has approximately double the depth of Chi-X, BATS, or Turquoise. Depth at the top of the book in shares is lower than in the United Kingdom for large-cap stocks and stable between 2012 and 2014 at approximately 1,200 shares, compared with a mean of 3,000 shares in the United Kingdom in 2014. Interestingly, top-of-book depth appears similar for small-cap stocks and large-cap stocks, at about 1,200 shares. Nevertheless, in value terms, depth for large-cap stocks is at least double that of small-cap stocks. The amount of depth in value terms is similar to that for the United Kingdom, with large-cap top depth in value terms increasing from a mean of EUR23,000 in 2012 to more than EUR36,000 in 2014 (compared with a mean of GBP24,000 for large-cap stocks in the United Kingdom in 2014).

The proportion of dark trades in France in large-cap stocks is about 4%, although it is skewed by the dominant Euronext being pretrade transparent. Disaggregated by exchange (not shown), the data show about 15% of trading on BATS in the dark in 2014 (compared with 10% in 2012); Chi-X and Turquoise have experienced a relatively stable 4% dark share.

In summary, the French market exhibits some similarities to the UK market but of note is the apparently larger depth in terms of shares and in terms of value in large-cap stocks at the top of the book, resulting in noticeably lower depth-weighted spreads. The French and UK markets are quite different, however, in terms of the number of stocks and the types of stocks, which makes any causal inferences about liquidity provision difficult on the basis of descriptive statistics alone.

Exhibit 3. Descriptive Statistics for French Data

	2012		2014	
Statistic	Large Cap	Small Cap	Large Cap	Small Cap
Relative spread (bps)				
Mean	7.30	12.48	6.13	13.61
Median	6.15	9.91	5.19	11.60
Std. dev.	5.04	8.30	4.21	7.79
Depth-weighted spread (bps)				
Mean	11.94	19.36	9.35	18.45
Median	9.60	15.29	7.57	14.56
Std. dev.	8.50	11.58	6.89	10.59
Effective spread (bps)				
Mean	4.87	9.49	4.09	9.81
Median	3.78	6.67	3.29	8.16
Std. dev.	4.46	8.28	3.83	7.26
Depth at top of book				
Mean	1,196	1,216	1,299	1,139
Median	576	716	540	618
Std. dev.	1,731	1,373	2,041	1,501
Depth (EUR value) at top of book				
Mean	23,260.95	13,408.88	36,095.85	14,568.28
Median	16,278.31	8,678.23	25,244.57	9,065.55
Std. dev.	21,507.01	13,212.34	32,489.68	16,088.74
Trade size				
Mean	278	334	246	352
Median	110	149	106	215
Std. dev.	453	475	384	410
Number of trades per day				
Mean	3,888	579	3,188	321
Median	2,586	26	2,568	6
Std. dev.	2,206	1,084	2,902	1,393

(continued)

Exhibit 3. Descriptive Statistics for French Data (continued)

	2012		2014	
Statistic	Large Cap	Small Cap	Large Cap	Small Cap
Quote-to-trade ratio				
Mean	64.8	215.10	43.48	99.78
Median	54.64	52.08	40.57	43.49
Std. dev.	35.53	539.15	15.95	157.20
Dark percent				
Mean	4.82%	1.91%	5.50%	2.05%
Median	4.17	0.00	3.45	0.00
Std. dev.	4.23	4.32	6.08	3.64

Note: The French market is aggregated across the Euronext, Chi-X, Turquoise, and BATS venues. Statistics are presented by market capitalisation with membership of each group determined by the CAC 40 Index in which the stock trades. The depth-weighted spread is based on executing an order for EUR25,000 worth of stock.

4.3. US Market

Exhibit 4 provides descriptive data for the US market. The data have been censored or winsorized at the 2% level so that any data above the 98th percentile were set equal to the value of the 98th percentile.

The spreads are smaller in the US than in the UK market; the median relative spread is 2.5–3.0 bps for large-cap stocks and 9–11 bps for small-cap stocks between 2010 and 2014. Relative to 2004, large-cap relative spreads have fallen by around 1 bp and small-cap spreads have almost halved. The change is even more apparent when these figures are compared with those for 1999. In 1999, relative spreads for large-cap stocks were around 20–25 bps (compared with 2–3 bps in 2014) and for small-cap stocks relative spreads were about 85–100 bps compared with 8–9 bps in 2014. Relative spreads appear to have come down by a factor of 10 in the past 15 years, although the vast majority of this decrease happened by 2004, which suggests that the rise of algorithmic and dark trading after Reg NMS has not been as important as the decimalisation and increased competition leading to Reg NMS. Effective spreads are similar to the relative spreads except that they are typically slightly less, reflecting the ability to achieve price improvement off-exchange.

Exhibit 4. Descriptive Statistics for US Data

	1999		2004		2010		2011		2014	
Statistic	Large Cap	Small Cap	Large Cap	Small Cap	Large Cap	Small Cap	Large Cap	Small Cap	Large Cap	Small Cap
Relative spread (bps)										
Mean	25.21	85.02	5.29	19.84	3.81	9.74	3.45	9.85	2.96	8.47
Median	21.04	100.92	3.82	27.54	2.95	10.58	2.46	11.08	2.27	8.82
Std. dev.	18.17	25.35	4.63	11.16	2.44	2.09	2.41	2.71	2.10	1.53
Effective spread (bps)										
Mean	26.94	132.44	8.46	75.44	3.77	7.18	3.39	6.12	2.88	7.82
Median	18.81	92.40	3.43	16.28	3.01	9.11	2.30	7.76	2.01	9.09
Std. dev.	58.26	143.22	51.36	349.38	2.79	3.60	2.65	3.45	2.39	2.69
Top-of-book depth										
Mean	3,337	1,003	1,631	387	32,948	368	42,831	332	32,034	312
Median	1,584	564	1,054	203	5,550	249	6,023	207	3,498	200
Std. dev.	4,303	1,118	1,745	599	72,724	592	95,003	618	75,965	490
Depth (USD value) at top of book										
Mean	175,230.40	25,057.50	59,197.30	12,951.50	540,894.70	11,461.90	713,951.80	11,465.70	619,102.40	13,983.30
Median	82,865.70	12,019.20	38,870.20	6,202.60	186,423.30	7,257.00	218,881.10	7,843.80	157,079.20	10,389.10
Std. dev.	237,492.80	28,618.20	62,596.00	23,453.30	944,790.50	17,204.70	1,286,099.20	9,574.40	1,236,316.10	8,096.20
Trade size										
Mean	988	732	425	310	256	151	265	166	195	118
Median	390	391	199	155	100	100	100	100	100	100
Std. dev.	1,827	1280	650	503	360	194	384	229	285	193
Number of trades per day										
Mean	1,095	13	5,618	87	34,965	276	28,821	285	30,191	105
Median	522	7	4,305	21	19,929	13	11,428	9	18,130	64
Std. dev.	1,745	16	7,184	191	33,652	408	22,882	370	38,400	147

(continued)

Exhibit 4. Descriptive Statistics for US Data (cotinued)

	1999		2004		2010		2011		2014	
Statistic	Large Cap	Small Cap	Large Cap	Small Cap	Large Cap	Small Cap	Large Cap	Small Cap	Large Cap	Small Cap
Quote-to-trade ratio										
Mean	2.521	4.125	6.4	42.208	15.053	44.069	15.757	98.19	15.791	76.785
Median	2.653	3.622	6.332	12.64	15.112	30.18	13.712	39.017	15.994	26.218
Std. dev.	1.738	3.071	1.456	50.67	3.625	42.745	5.042	206.115	3.825	181.615
Dark percent										
Mean	na	na	na	na	19.65%	19.96%	18.30%	19.80%	21.63%	33.92%
Median	na	na	na	na	19.06	16.35	18.01	19.51	20.86	28.32
Std. dev.	na	na	na	na	4.24	11.06	3.79	6.35	4.31	13.75

Notes: Statistics for the US market are aggregated across all trading venues that report to SIP. Statistics are presented by market capitalisation; the full list of stocks is available on request.

na = not available.

Depth in terms of shares and also in value terms (hereafter, dollar depth) exhibits an inverted U shape over the sample period, with the median large-cap depth rising from 5,500 shares (USD186,000) in 2010 to 6,000 shares (USD219,000) in 2011 before falling again to 3,500 shares (USD157,000) in 2014. The median trade size for both small- and large-cap stocks has remained flat at the standard lot size of 100 shares. The depth statistics are noticeably higher in 2010–2014 than in 2004 and 1999, when median top-of-book depth was, respectively, 1,000–1,500 shares (USD39,000–USD83,000).

The quote-to-trade ratio has been stable at about 15 for large-cap stocks, but the small-cap quote-to-trade ratio has been more volatile during this time (between 25 and 40). Compared with 1999 and 2004, when the median quote-to-trade ratio was, respectively, 2.7 and 6.3, quoting activity (relative to trading activity) has increased dramatically, reflecting the rise of algorithmic trading strategies.

Finally, the proportion of dark trading in large-cap stocks increased slightly over the sample period—from almost 19% to almost 21%. Small-cap stocks experienced a large increase in the proportion of dark trading, particularly after 2011, from around 19% to 27% of trades. Because off-exchange trading has been reported to the FINRA/NASDAQ Trade Reporting Facility only since 2009, establishing any accurate statistics about off-exchange trading before this time is difficult.

In summary, the descriptive statistics for the United States suggest the following stylized facts:

- Spreads are lower than in the United Kingdom and France, although institutional trading costs could not be estimated via depth-weighted spreads.
- Dark trading as a proportion of all trading has increased by 1.5–2.0 percentage points and is significantly higher than in the United Kingdom (20%–30% in the United States compared with 5%–7% in the United Kingdom).[9]

[9]Note, however, that the comparison of dark trading proportions is not direct. The US dark trading data are based on the consolidated tape, which captures all dark trades reported to a FINRA trade-reporting facility. In the United Kingdom, only those dark trades reported to the venues analysed could be captured. Europe currently has no equivalent consolidated tape system and thus no single repository for dark trade reporting.

5. Analysis

The analysis here first addresses adverse selection on lit markets, including how the stable quote periods were identified. This analysis is divided between US data and UK/French data. This section then turns to the impact of trades on the order book.

5.1. Adverse Selection on Lit Markets

Adverse selection on lit markets is an issue often raised by practitioners when voicing concerns about modern market structure. Adverse selection may increase the risk that a market maker will lose money to informed traders and, therefore, cause market makers to raise their spreads to counter this risk. Non-HFT investors may therefore face higher direct trading costs than HFTs.

One manifestation of adverse selection is that during periods of stable prices, trading has been conducted primarily on dark trading venues (or via internalization), allowing HFT internalizers to capture the spread by offering only nominal price improvement. The majority of lit quotes appear to be executed against only when the computer algorithms are able to predict, on the basis of such factors as order-book imbalance, that a given quote is about to roll. In this way, lit quotes are adversely selected against. Recall from earlier sections that increased adverse selection on lit exchanges may disincentivise displayed liquidity provision or deter investors from using lit markets entirely, thereby negatively affecting price formation and market quality (Kwan, Masulis, and McInish 2015).

This scenario was analysed through creation of a dashboard of metrics, presented in **Exhibit 5**, which provides a snapshot of trading during a particular time period for the stock of Bank of America (BAC) on 6 June 2014. The time of interest is between 13:25 and 13:31, when the quote was stable at 15.62–15.63 (apart from a temporary change down to 15.61–15.62 around 13:30). The scenario of concern can be seen most dramatically in Panel G, "Number of Lit Trades," where a clear spike in trades on lit markets occurs just before the quote rolls down and then again just before the quote rolls up.

Similarly, Panel D, "Log of Lit Buy/Sell Size," shows a concentration of squares (representing sell trades in lit markets) around the time of the quote rolling down, followed by a concentration of circles (representing buy trades in lit markets) around the time of the subsequent roll up. The amount of quoting activity also spikes at the times of the quote rolls (which can be seen in Panel F, "Number of Quotes"). As expected, the amount of

Exhibit 5. Visual Example of Adverse Selection: Bank of America, 6 June 2014

A. NBBO-BAC

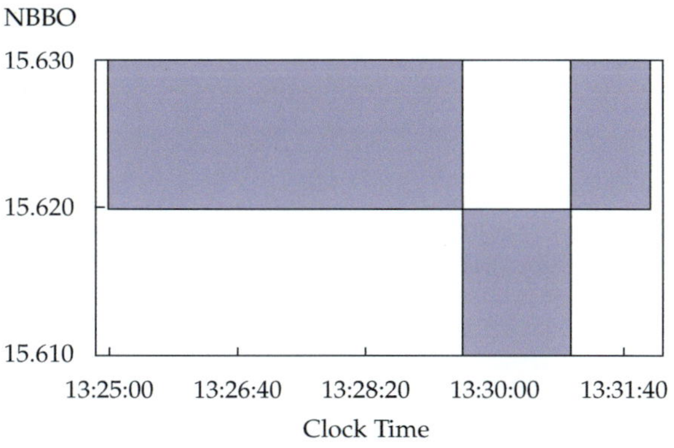

B. NBBO Bid and Offer Sizes

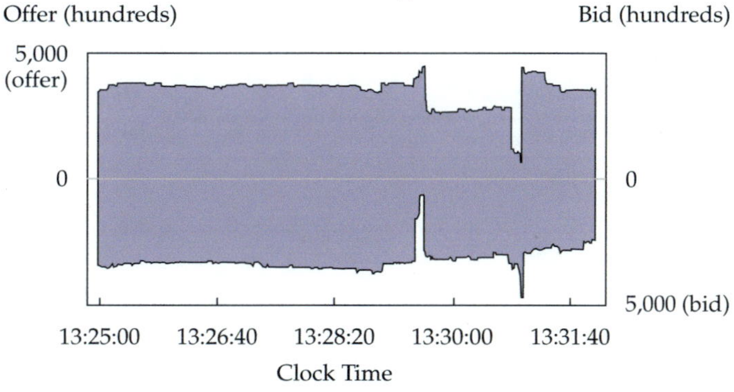

C. Lit Trading Proportion over Last 5 sec.

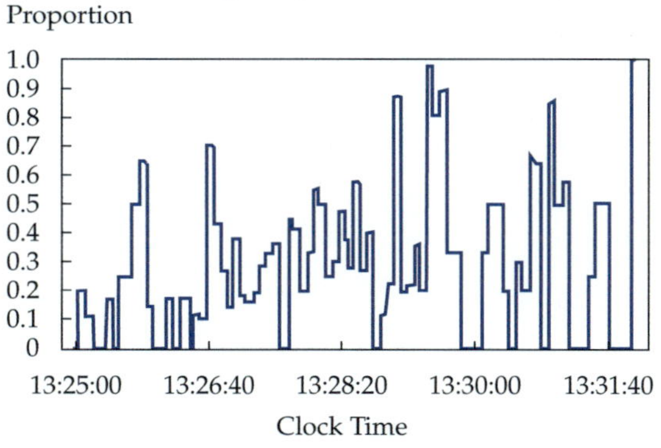

(continued)

Exhibit 5. Visual Example of Adverse Selection: Bank of America, 6 June 2014 (continued)

D. Log of Lit Buy/Sell Size

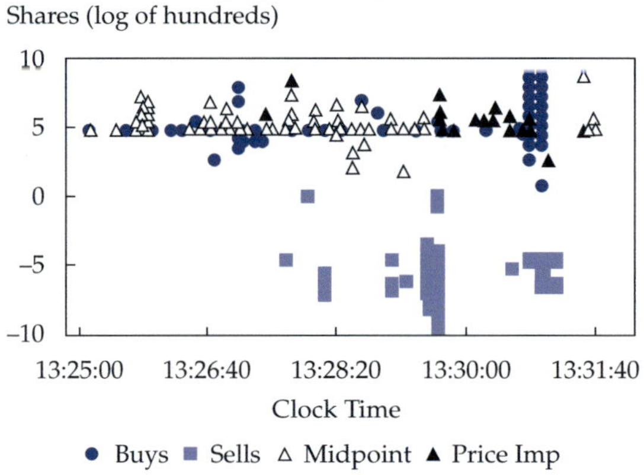

E. Log of Dark Buy/Sell Size

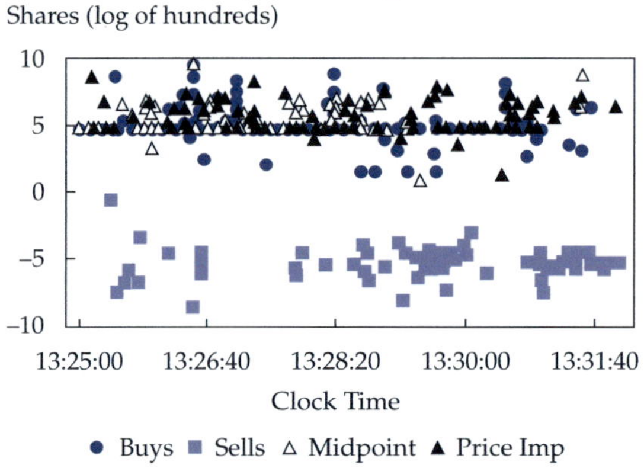

F. Number of Quotes in Previous 500 ms.

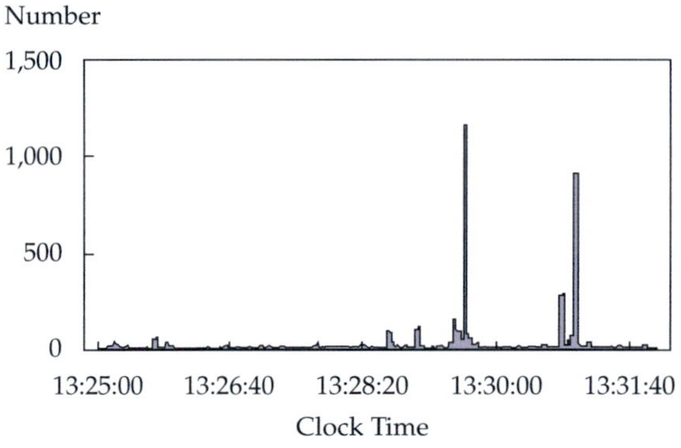

(continued)

Exhibit 5. Visual Example of Adverse Selection: Bank of America, 6 June 2014 (continued)

G. Number of Lit Trades in Previous 500 ms.

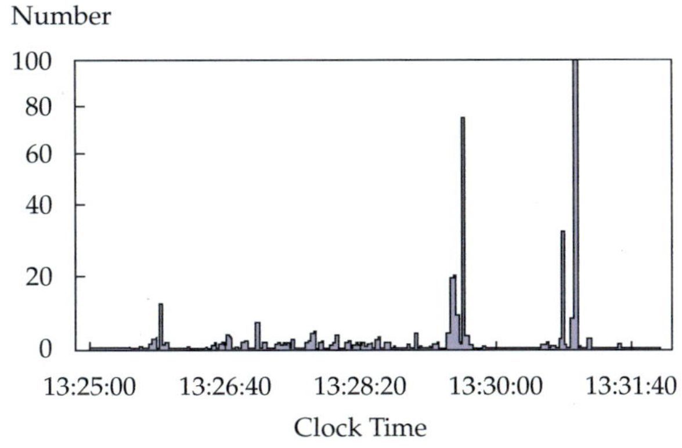

H. Number of Dark Trades in Previous 500 ms.

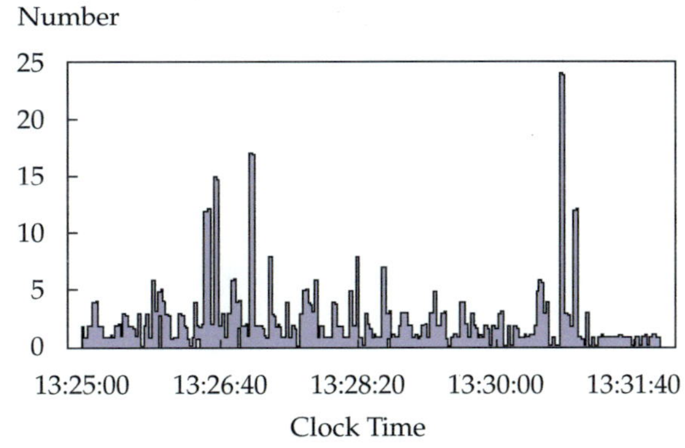

I. Net Buying Interest

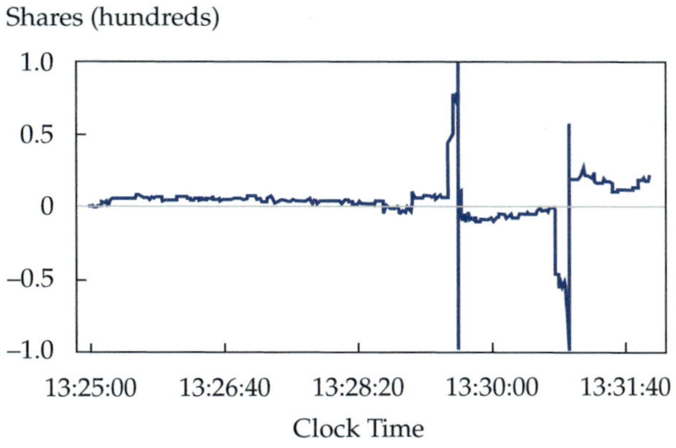

dark trading stays relatively stable at about five trades per 500 milliseconds throughout the sample period except for some spikes around 13:26 that are unrelated to the quote roll and a spike just after the second quote roll (shown in Panel H, "Number of Dark Trades").

Panel I, "Net Buying Interest," shows a measure of the difference between offer and bid depths divided by total depth. This measure approaches 1 (i.e., the bid depth goes to zero, leading up to the quote rolling down) before subsequently approaching –1 (i.e., the offer depth goes to zero leading up to the quote rolling up).

This pattern can also be seen in Panel B, "NBBO Bid and Offer Sizes," where two discontinuities appear in the otherwise uniform shaded area. The first is the bid-side depth (plotted as the area below the $y = 0$ line) approaching zero before being reestablished at the lower bid price. This phenomenon is followed by a discontinuity on the offer side (plotted as the area above the $y = 0$ line), which approaches zero before being reestablished at the higher offer price.

Identifying Stable Quote Periods

To isolate times of quote stability, I looked for runs of unchanging bids and offers that lasted for at least 1,000 quote updates. The period of each run was defined as a stable period; any period that was not a stable period was considered one in which the quote was rolling. **Exhibit 6** shows the length in clock time of the isolated stable periods. It shows that in the United States, the median stable period lasted about five minutes in 2014, down from eight minutes in 2010.

The United Kingdom has experienced no obvious trend, with the stable quote lasting around six minutes, although as can be seen in the "Periods" column, the frequency with which a quote remained stable was less than in the United States by a factor of 10–20. France had even fewer stable quote periods—to the point that any further analysis is not possible for the French market. The existence of relatively lengthy periods of time for which the quote did not move is consistent with an artificial constraint on market activity that prevents the equilibrium price from being accurately obtained in lit venues. The effect is to cause trading to move off-exchange where price improvement at subtick increments is possible.

US Analysis

Exhibit 7 shows the proportion of US trades that were dark in stable and nonstable periods. The results suggest that during periods of quote stability, for large-cap stocks, about 32%–34% of trading occurs in the dark, compared with 16%–20% when the quote is not

Exhibit 6. Statistics of Stable Quote Periods

Country	Year	Periods	Length of Stable Quote Period (minutes)	
			Median	Std. Dev.
United States	2010	24,298	8.3	106.8
	2011	15,480	5.5	97.0
	2014	42,716	4.9	94.7
United Kingdom	2010	1,134	5.5	53.9
	2012	810	9.8	60.6
	2014	640	6.0	34.3
France	2012	628	1.1	57.2
	2014	200	2.9	70.8

Note: The "Periods" column documents the number of stable quote periods identified for each market.

stable or rolling. This difference is statistically significant at the 1% level. The same consistent effect is not observed for small-cap stocks.

Specifically, for small-cap stocks, the proportion of dark trading during nonstable quote periods rose gradually from 16% in 2010 to 21% in 2011 and to 26% in 2014. However, the proportion of dark trading during stable periods increased dramatically between 2010–2011 and 2014—from 10% to 36%. The number of such stable periods identified also rose dramatically—from 27 in 2010 to more than 800 in 2014—whereas the number of nonstable periods remained relatively constant.

These observations are consistent with the spread-capturing internalization strategy being gradually expanded into the small-cap market after being initially deployed in the large-cap market. This pattern may also be consistent with the rise in median trades per day for small-cap stocks shown in Exhibit 4—from about 10 in 2010–2011 to 64 in 2014. If so, then the results for 2014 show that the adverse selection effect has migrated to the small-cap market because the proportion of dark trading during stable quote periods is significantly higher than during nonstable periods.

Exhibit 7. Quote Rolls and Dark Trading in US Markets

Year	Market Cap	Period	Number of Observations	Mean	Std. Dev.	p-Value
2010	Large	Nonstable	11,572,509	17.65%	38.12%	
		Stable	4,832,933	32.38	46.79	
		Difference		14.73***	40.87	<0.0001
	Small	Nonstable	82,951	16.08	36.74	
		Stable	27	11.11	32.03	
		Difference		–4.97	36.74	0.4273
2011	Large	Nonstable	6,873,556	16.25%	36.89%	
		Stable	2,971,540	32.71	46.91	
		Difference		16.46***	40.18	<0.0001
	Small	Nonstable	98,090	20.61	40.45	
		Stable	224	10.27	30.42	
		Difference		–10.35***	40.43	<0.0001
2014	Large	Nonstable	12,968,844	20.19%	40.14%	
		Stable	5,564,786	34.33	47.48	
		Difference		14.15***	42.48	<0.0001
	Small	Nonstable	92,061	25.55	43.62	
		Stable	815	35.83	47.98	
		Difference		10.28***	43.66	<0.0001

Notes: The exhibit shows results of difference-in-means tests for the proportion of dark trading as a percentage of all trading during stable and nonstable quote periods. The p-value is presented for the difference-in-means test. The "Number of Observations" column shows the number of quote messages for each period type. The "Std. Dev." column shows the standard deviation of the proportion of dark trading for each period type.

***Significant at the 1% level.

UK and French Analyses

The same analysis for the consolidated UK market (not shown) revealed no statistically significant difference in the amount of dark trading between stable and nonstable periods. But this finding is accompanied by several caveats. First, because of no consolidated tape or trade-through protection in the United Kingdom, the strategy of quote leaning during stable periods before executing against lit orders when the quote rolls may be, at best, an exchange-by-exchange proposition.

Exhibit 8, which shows this venue-by-venue analysis for the BATS, Chi-X, and Turquoise exchanges (recall that the LSE does not operate a dark order book), indicates an increase in the proportion of dark trading for these three exchanges, although the statistical significance is not uniform across all cases.

The strongest results are for the BATS exchange, where, as in the United States, dark trading during stable quote periods was more than double that occurring in nonstable periods during 2010–2012. Interestingly, 2012 coincided with a tightening of the interpretation of UK payment-for-order-flow rules, which effectively resulted in the practice being banned. The ability to pay for and internalize order flow is consistent with the quote-roll strategy as described previously, so the interruption of this effect in 2014 may be related to the regime change. The statistical significance of the tests for Chi-X and Turquoise venues, however, does not appear consistent with this interpretation.

This type of analysis was repeated for the French market (not shown), but similar patterns were not seen. Apart from the Chi-X venue in 2012 and Turquoise in 2014, insufficient instances of stable quote periods were found to make any statistical inferences, and for these two examples, I found no statistically significant difference in dark trading proportions between stable and nonstable periods (Chi-X in 2012) and a statistically significant reduction in dark trading during stable quote periods (Turquoise in 2014).

A reasonable conclusion is that the practice of leaning on the quotes during stable quote periods and then executing against lit venues as the quote is about to roll is a mostly US phenomenon, particularly in large-cap stocks. This manifestation of adverse selection could be interpreted as the consequence of the differing market structures between the United States and Europe. The consolidated-tape and trade-through rules most likely make it simpler for algorithms to predict quote rolls, although as seen in the limited UK evidence, the process can apparently be ported over to individual exchanges and markets with no consolidated tape.

The fact that the phenomenon appears to exist mostly for large-cap US stocks, which typically all trade at the minimum one-tick spread for large parts of the trading day, may also have implications for policy discussions about changing tick sizes. The price improvement strategy is probably possible because the lit venues are not able to offer spreads any lower than 1 tick, even for stocks where the equilibrium spread is likely smaller. Order flow is, therefore, attracted more easily and in more volume to dark venues that can offer subpenny price improvement and greater execution certainty, which increases adverse selection for order flow remaining on lit exchanges. By increasing tick sizes in the hope of pooling more liquidity in fewer tick "buckets," authorities may make this problem more acute.

Exhibit 8. Quote Rolls and Dark Trading in UK Markets, by Exchange

Year	Venue	Period	Number of Observations	Mean	Std. Dev.	*p*-Value
2010	BATS Europe	Nonstable	481,601	5.10%	21.99%	
		Stable	1,115	17.94	38.38	
		Difference		12.84***	22.05	<0.0001
	Chi-X	Nonstable	1,103,726	3.37	18.04	
		Stable	10,004	6.32	24.33	
		Difference		2.95***	18.11	<0.0001
	Turquoise	Nonstable	304,929	12.17	32.69	
		Stable	392	9.95	29.97	
		Difference		–2.22	32.69	0.1435
2012	BATS Europe	Nonstable	382,714	8.71%	28.20%	
		Stable	570	20.70	40.55	
		Difference		11.99***	28.23	<0.0001
	Chi-X	Nonstable	1,323,628	4.82	21.41	
		Stable	6,506	5.66	23.10	
		Difference		0.84	21.42	0.35
	Turquoise	Nonstable	281,985	5.10	22.00	
		Stable	2,412	12.56	33.15	
		Difference		7.46***	22.12	<0.0001
2014	BATS Europe	Nonstable	510,345	13.97%	34.67%	
		Stable	153	17.65	38.25	
		Difference		3.68	34.67	0.2360
	Chi-X	Nonstable	1,408,496	7.13	25.73	
		Stable	514	14.40	35.14	
		Difference		7.27***	25.73	<0.0001
	Turquoise	Nonstable	1,005,518	6.60	24.82	
		Stable	589	11.88	32.39	
		Difference		5.29***	24.83	<0.0001

(continued)

Exhibit 8. Quote Rolls and Dark Trading in UK Markets, by Exchange (continued)

Notes: The exhibit shows results of difference-in-means tests for the proportion of dark trading as a percentage of all trading during stable and nonstable quote periods. The *p*-value is presented for the difference-in-means test. The "Number of Observations" column shows the number of quote messages for each period type. The "Std. Dev." column shows the standard deviation of the proportion of dark trading for each period type.

***Significant at the 1% level.

5.2. Trade Impact on the Order Book

Another concern, in addition to adverse selection, that is frequently voiced about the rise of high-frequency traders relates to the concept of phantom liquidity. Many investment professionals have commented that quoted depth at the top of the book is no longer a good measure of the true depth of the market. HFTs often post liquidity in multiple venues to increase the probability of execution. Once one of the limit orders executes, the HFTs quickly cancel the other orders, so the original quoted depth was overestimating the true liquidity provision (van Kervel 2012).

To estimate the size of this phenomenon, the amount of depth lost at the top of the book in the immediate aftermath of a trade was measured. All trades were isolated to provide an estimate of the order-book impact of a trade; then, the depth at the top of the book was identified a minimum of 50 milliseconds after the trade. The findings are shown in **Exhibit 9**, where order-book message $n + m$ is the first order-book message more than 50 milliseconds away from the trade (which is order-book message n). The notation $n + m$ makes explicit that a variable number of messages may be recorded between the two events. Similarly, the actual amount of clock time elapsed between message n and message $n + m$ is variable but greater than 50 milliseconds.

Exhibit 9. Variable Definitions for Analysis of Trade Impact

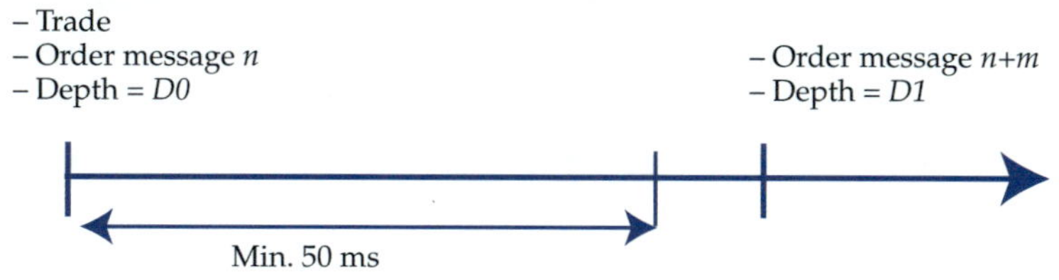

The null hypothesis was that when a trade occurs, an amount of depth equal to the size of the trade should disappear from the book—that is, size of trade = $D0 - D1$. If this size is divided by the size of the trade, it produces the quantity called "Trade impact" = $(D0 - D1)$/Size, which should have a value of 1 under the null hypothesis. The alternative hypothesis of phantom liquidity would be consistent with a trade of size X removing, say, 2X from the order book as other orders are cancelled.

Panel A of **Exhibit 10** shows for the UK market (excluding the pretrade transparent LSE) statistics for the trade impact variable. The top-of-the-book depth was measured a minimum of 50 milliseconds after the trade. In Panel A, we see no statistically significant difference in the impact of a trade on order-book depth between stable and nonstable quote periods in any of the years.

Exhibit 10. Impact of a Trade on Top-Level Order-Book Depth: UK Data

	Period	Class	Number of Observations	Mean	Std. Dev.	*p*-Value
A. BATS Europe, Chi-X, and Turquoise venues						
	2010	Nonstable	746,629	0.9205	1.2372	
		Stable	4,508	0.9424	1.6317	
		Difference		−0.0219	1.2399	0.5807
	2012	Nonstable	489,043	1.0698	1.3285	
		Stable	3,511	0.9533	1.7961	
		Difference		0.1165	1.3324	0.1577
	2014	Nonstable	545,209	1.1948	1.3141	
		Stable	1,091	1.3847	1.6114	
		Difference		−0.1899	1.3148	0.3468
B. LSE						
	2010		337,740	0.5642	1.2198	
	2012		232,912	0.9437	1.3375	
	2014		239,733	1.2047	1.3095	

Notes: A stable period is defined as one where the quote does not change for at least 1,000 quote messages. The *p*-value is for the difference-in-means *t*-test.

Panel B, which shows the aggregate trade impact for the LSE alone, indicates that the average trade impact was increasing between 2010 and 2014—from 0.5× the size of the trade to 1.2×.

The histograms of trade impacts in the UK market that are shown in **Exhibit 11** shed more light on these statistics. Panels A, B, and C show the histograms for trades on the LSE only in, respectively, 2010, 2012, and 2014. The rest of the panels show trade impacts for Chi-X, Turquoise, and BATS Europe for nonstable periods (Panels D, E, and F) and stable periods (Panels G, H, and I). A stable period was defined as one in which the best quote did not change for at least 1,000 quote messages.

The trade impact histograms for the LSE in Exhibit 11 have a bimodal form; that is, the majority of trades had an impact on the top of the order book either equal to the size of the trade (trade impact ratio = 1) or of zero magnitude (trade impact ratio = 0). This finding means that a trade took out an amount of top-of-the-book depth equal to its size or no depth at all (i.e., the amount traded was immediately replaced at the top of the book). The mode at zero may be surprising; it suggests that the top of the order book is resilient to trades and replaces liquidity very quickly—that is, within 50 or so milliseconds, the amount of depth taken out by an order of a given size has already been replaced at the top of the book.

Panels A, B, and C do not reveal any significant changes for the LSE between 2010, 2012, and 2014 other than the trade impact density increasing at 1 and reducing at 0 in 2014, which explains the mean trade impact increasing from 0.5× to 1.2× as discussed previously. Specifically, although approximately 50% of trades on the LSE had an impact of 0 in 2010–2012, this number had decreased to below 10% by 2014. This pattern may suggest that liquidity is not being replaced on the LSE as quickly as it once was. This finding, combined with the fact that no obvious changes are seen in Panels G–I for the Chi-X, BATS, and Turquoise markets, is consistent with the concern that liquidity provision in lit venues may be disincentivised under the current market structure.

The US results shown in **Exhibit 12** are quite different from the UK results but are consistent with US markets being more liquid. The trade impact distribution has only one mode, centered on 0, and almost 100% of trades had no impact on the order book. There is little evidence of change in these metrics between 2010, 2011, and 2014.

Exhibit 11. Trade Impacts: UK Data

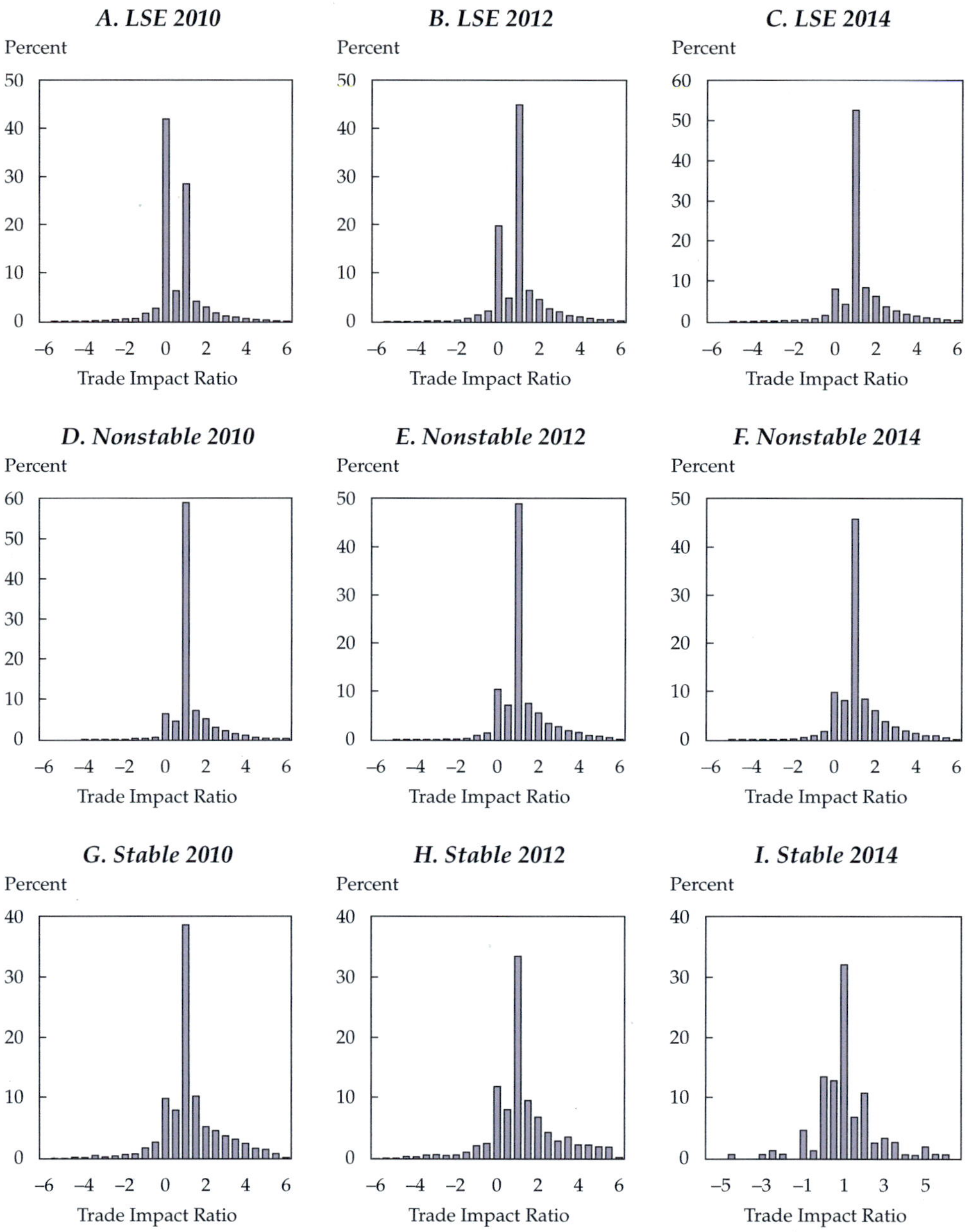

Exhibit 12. Trade Impacts: US Data

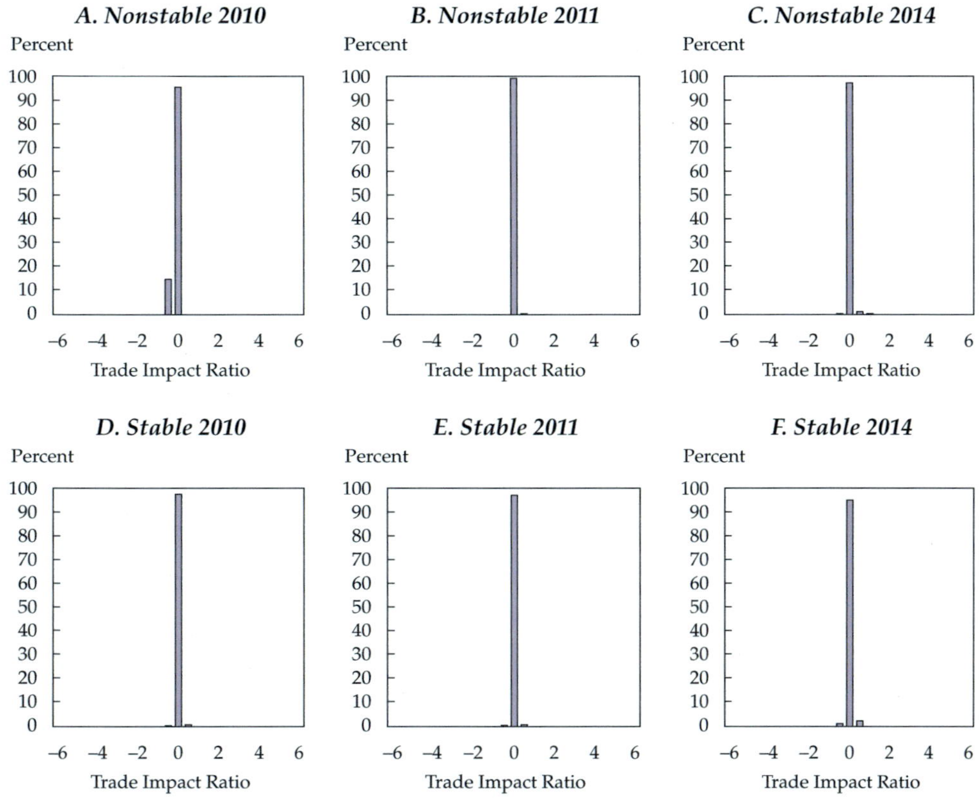

Notes: Trade impact was calculated and top-of-the-book depth was measured as previously. A stable period is one in which the best quote did not change for at least 1,000 quote messages.

6. Conclusion

To address some practitioner concerns about modern equity market structure, this study investigated two issues surrounding adverse selection and liquidity resilience in the US, UK, and French equity markets. First, adverse selection issues on lit markets were examined by estimating the ability of electronic market makers to selectively interact with lit venues only when they are on the right side of the trade. Specifically, the issue is whether OTC market makers predict when the quote is about to roll and route their own orders to lit venues, where they trade in the direction of expected price changes. In this case, displayed liquidity providers would be adversely selected against and end up being on the wrong side of the trade. The study found evidence consistent with the phenomenon of OTC market makers offering price improvement and capturing the spread during stable quote periods before executing against lit orders when they can predict the quote is about to roll. This phenomenon was observed mainly in the United States, although it appears to be present on a venue-by-venue basis in the United Kingdom. It does not appear to feature in France.

These findings are consistent with the set of US equity market incentives—trade-through protection, retail internalization, and the consolidated quote and tape system—having the undesirable side effect of OTC market makers being likely to trade on lit venues only when they are better informed. Despite this clear example of adverse selection in action, however, no noticeable reduction in market quality appears to have occurred in terms of direct trading costs. This problem does not appear to exist to the same extent in European markets, with their different market incentives, although it can be observed on a venue-by-venue basis in the United Kingdom, particularly for large-cap stocks prior to 2012 (perhaps coinciding with the Financial Conduct Authority's strict reaffirming of payment-for-order-flow rules that year).

These findings have implications for tick size policy. The quote-roll phenomenon is found mostly in large-cap US stocks, which typically trade at the minimum 1 tick spread for large parts of the trading day. The price-improvement/quote-roll strategy is enabled by lit venues not being able to offer spreads any lower than 1 tick. Order flow is thus more easily and in more volume attracted to dark venues, which can offer subpenny price improvement and greater execution certainty. The effect is to increase adverse selection for order flow remaining on lit exchanges. The SEC is conducting a pilot program that increases tick sizes in the small-cap market to see whether liquidity will "pool" in fewer tick buckets. The findings of this study suggest, however, that such a change might cause the quote-roll strategy to become more widespread, which would likely increase adverse selection.

Second, the study estimated the extent to which depth at the top of the order book may be composed of duplicate liquidity by examining the impact of a trade on the order-book depth in terms of a multiple of the trade size. The study found no evidence that the trade impact in the United States has changed between 2010 and 2014. With the immediate trade impact found to be zero, this finding reflects the deep liquidity of US markets. Some evidence was found, however, that the trade impact in the dominant UK lit venue, the LSE, has worsened over time; liquidity is being replaced more slowly in 2014 than in 2010–2012.

These findings suggest that the overall state of liquidity in modern markets, as measured by most traditional metrics, is good. A focus on adverse selection risk by policymakers is warranted, however, to avoid further disincentivising participation in lit markets. Although documenting negative effects on aggregate liquidity metrics is difficult, instances of systematic adverse selection in lit venues can be observed. This issue should be addressed to ensure that market participants retain confidence in the integrity of markets.

References

Alampieski, K., and A. Lepone. 2011. "High Frequency Trading Firms, Order Book Participation and Liquidity Supply during Periods of Heightened Adverse Selection Risk: Evidence from LSE, BATS and Chi-X." Working paper: www.ecmcrc.org/Articles/High_Frequency_Trading_firms,orderbook_participation_and_liquidity_supply_during_periods_of_heightened_adverse_selection_risk-Evidence_from_LSE,BATS_and_Chi-X.pdf.

Bershova, N., and D. Rakhlink. 2013. "High-Frequency Trading and Long-Term Investors: A View from the Buy-Side." *Journal of Investment Strategies*, vol. 2, no. 2 (Spring): 25–69.

Brogaard, J., T. Hendershott, and R. Riordan. 2013. "High Frequency Trading and Price Discovery." European Central Bank Working Paper Series No. 1602 (22 April).

Carrion, A. 2013. "Very Fast Money: High-Frequency Trading on the NASDAQ." *Journal of Financial Markets*, vol. 16, no. 4 (November): 680–711.

Degryse, H., F. De Jong, and V. van Kervel. 2015. "The Impact of Dark Trading and Visible Fragmentation on Market Quality." *Review of Finance*, vol. 19, no. 4 (July): 1587–1622.

Foley, S., and T. Putnins. 2014. "Regulatory Efforts to Reduce Dark Trading in Canada and Australia: How Have They Worked?" Working paper (2 October).

Gao, C., and B. Mizrach. 2013. "Market Quality Breakdowns in Equities." Working paper (11 February).

Hendershott, T., C.M. Jones, and A.J. Menkveld. 2011. "Does Algorithmic Trading Improve Liquidity?" *Journal of Finance*, vol. 66, no. 1 (February): 1–33.

Hendershott, T., and H. Mendelson. 2000. "Crossing Networks and Dealer Markets: Competition and Performance." *Journal of Finance*, vol. 55, no. 5 (October): 2071–2115.

Jones, C. 2013. "What Do We Know about High-Frequency Trading?" Working paper, Columbia Business School Research Paper No. 13-11 (20 March).

Jovanovic, B., and A. Menkveld. 2011. "Middlemen in Limit-Order Markets." Working paper, Western Finance Association.

Kirilenko, A., A. Kyle, M. Samadi, and T. Tuzun. 2014. "The Flash Crash: The Impact of High Frequency Trading on an Electronic Market." Working paper (24 September).

Kwan, A., R. Masulis, and T. McInish. 2015. "Trading Rules, Competition for Order Flow and Market Fragmentation." *Journal of Financial Economics*, vol. 115, no. 2 (February): 330–348.

Madhavan, A. 2012. "Exchange-Traded Funds, Market Structure, and the Flash Crash." *Financial Analysts Journal*, vol. 68, no. 4 (July/August): 20–35.

Menkveld, A. 2013. "High Frequency Trading and the New Market Makers." *Journal of Financial Markets*, vol. 16, no. 4 (November): 712–740.

Preece, R. 2012. *Dark Pools, Internalization, and Equity Market Quality*. Charlottesville, VA: CFA Institute.

Preece, R., and S. Rosov. 2014. "Dark Trading and Equity Market Quality." *Financial Analysts Journal*, vol. 70, no. 6 (November/December): 33–48.

SEC. 2014. "Equity Market Structure Literature Review, Part II: High Frequency Trading" (18 March): www.sec.gov/marketstructure/research/hft_lit_review_march_2014.pdf.

Tong, L. 2013. "A Blessing or a Curse? The Impact of High Frequency Trading on Institutional Investors." Working paper.

van Kervel, V. 2012. "Liquidity: What You See Is What You Get?" Working paper (April).

Zhang, S.S. 2012. "Need for Speed: An Empirical Analysis of Hard and Soft Information in a High Frequency World." Working paper (30 July).

Zhu, H. 2014. "Do Dark Pools Harm Price Discovery?" *Review of Financial Studies*, vol. 27, no. 3 (March): 747–789.

CFA Institute

AUTHOR

Sviatoslav Rosov, PhD, CFA
Analyst
Capital Markets Policy, EMEA

CONTRIBUTORS

Kurt N. Schacht, JD, CFA
Managing Director
Standards and Advocacy

Robert W. Dannhauser, FRM, CAIA, CFA
Head
Global Capital Markets Policy

Rhodri Preece, CFA
Head
Capital Markets Policy, EMEA

We would also like to thank Dennis Dick, CFA, who serves on the CFA Institute Capital Markets Policy Council, for helping to develop this study and for his insightful input.

Made in the USA
Monee, IL
05 November 2026

67377486R00033